# XV

Zach Goldberg

**NOMADIC PRESS**

**OAKLAND**
111 FAIRMOUNT AVENUE
OAKLAND, CA 94611

**BROOKLYN**
475 KENT AVENUE #302
BROOKLYN, NY 11249

WWW.NOMADICPRESS.ORG

**MASTHEAD**

*FOUNDING AND MANAGING EDITOR*
J. K. FOWLER

*ASSOCIATE EDITOR*
MICHAELA MULLIN

*DESIGN*
J. K. FOWLER

**MISSION STATEMENT**

Nomadic Press is a 501 (C)(3) not-for-profit organization that supports the works of emerging and established writers and artists. Through publications (including translations) and performances, Nomadic Press aims to build community among artists and across disciplines.

**SUBMISSIONS**

Nomadic Press wholeheartedly accepts unsolicited book manuscripts. To submit your work, please visit www.nomadicpress.org/submissions

**DISTRIBUTION**

Orders by trade bookstores and wholesalers:
Small Press Distribution,
1341 Seventh Street
Berkeley, CA 94701
spd@spdbooks.org
(510) 524-1668 / (800) 869-7553

**XV**


This book was made possible by a loving community of chosen family and friends, old and new.

For author questions or to book a reading at your bookstore, university/school, or alternative establishment, please send an email to info@nomadicpress.org.

Cover artwork and author portrait by Arthur Johnstone

Published by Nomadic Press, 111 Fairmount Avenue, Oakland, CA 94611

First printing, 2020

Printed in the United States of America

LIBRARY OF CONGRESS CATALOGING-IN-PUBLICATION DATA

Goldberg, Zach 1991 –
Title: *XV*
P. CM.
Summary: These poems want to blame someone. When the waters are unsettled, who or what is responsible? *XV* by Zach Goldberg probes concepts of masculinity, love, and trauma through the lens of inheritance. The body is a vessel for history, but what do we do with history? Ignore it? Deny it? Revise it? Heal from it?

[1. POETRY/LOVE. 2. POETRY/TRAUMA. 3. AMERICAN GENERAL.] I. III. TITLE.

LIBRARY OF CONGRESS CONTROL NUMBER: 2019957652

ISBN: 978-1-7344377-4-4

# XV

Zach Goldberg

NOMADIC
PRESS

# CONTENTS

# INTRODUCTION

In March of 2015, I woke up in a hospital bed. I had gone to the ER after several days of cardiac irregularities, and during a blood draw, I experienced an extreme episode of vasovagal syncope. My blood pressure dropped rapidly, I lost consciousness, and my heart stopped for fifteen seconds. Over the next several months, I developed an entirely new vocabulary to speak about my body and its shortcomings. My father and his father both experienced cardiac events as middle-aged men, and in the immediate aftermath of my health scare, it was tempting to see my medical problems as part of a larger story—something I was destined for. I wrote into this idea and dug up uncomfortable emotions: anger at my family for the inevitability of their genes, guilt that I had somehow failed my father, fear that I would never be able to escape my inheritance.

*XV* begins with this fear, but it doesn't end there. The work of putting this collection together allowed me to look at fear as an opportunity for grace, and as I filtered my experience through language, I arrived at some degree of compassion for my family, my sickness, and myself. *XV* is an exploration of the ways in which our parents live in us and the ways in which we live in them. Writing these poems was an exercise in learning to participate in a narrative without being consumed by it. I was able to come to an understanding of the body as a vessel carrying past traumas through time, but also the body as a single stone in one long river. We can't escape history, but we aren't entirely contained by it either. If trauma belongs to multiple generations, then so does the act of healing. Our only goal should be to make our children less sick than ourselves.

# SYNCOPE

It starts with a lie: That a little god
beats in the pit of me. What a sham it is
to grow up believing
in the pulse's sovereignty over the body.
Today, a machine registers the fiction
every time it surfaces, and I'm struck
by the gory truth that lies inside.
The barrier is paper-thin,
evidenced by blood as it billows
into a bag of saline. Watch it cloud the clear
liquid with its dark. Watch me empty myself
of myself. Perverse fluorescent hum.
Flesh's wicked reversal. I lie
in wait and the air chops roughly
as it makes its way. My mouth, lined
with steel wool. The room, wrapped tight
with gauze. What else is false?
Light is just a rumor, and I'm falling
through a trapdoor in the body.

## I. PHLEBOTOMY

It's only blood, she says, as if there were
 some other liquid I'd prefer to spill.
She says it's mostly salt and water. See
 how easily our families have turned
our bodies into oceans? Truth is that
 I don't much fear the needle anymore.
The act, benign and violent in its way.
 The bleeding I can live with, but what's worse
is picturing the push and pull, the way
 the heart will just as likely empty us
as make us full. I know it fluctuates.
 I know that blood is harmless, mostly salt
and water, but I never get to ask
 her what the rest of it is made of.

## II. INCANTATION

If I know anything about you
(and I do) it's that you didn't lose faith
until the first time you entered a church.
This says more about your sense of humor
than your skepticism, that you once shook
a holy man's hand with your fingers crossed
behind your back. That your name means Rock
though you move like water. I wonder
would you say God is benign
in the way a tumor is?

You know better than most of us
that we don't get all our words from books
or bodies. Good religion comes to us
when we need it most, even if we don't recognize it
(and we don't). Repetition is the key
to any successful ritual. It could be the mantra
I repeat every morning on my cushion.
The prayer poised on my tongue
as I drove you to the emergency room.

Prayer, which is nothing but the rope
that pulls a boat in for docking. It doesn't
make exceptions one way or the other,
not even for heretics. That day at the hospital
it made itself a knot around your bed.
It held against the current of the IV drip.
You can tell both where a liquid is going
and where it comes from. Maybe that's why
years later, I followed you down the river.
You are a tradition. You were and are still
practiced. You are practicing.

Dear father, where do you think I went
for those fifteen seconds? Where were you?
This is to say, though you never put your hands
together, never said the words, still
I am here. Like you, every bit a skeptic,
but if I've learned one thing from religion
(and I have), it's that you can conjure
the memory of a man into the world
merely by repeating his name.

## III. EVERYTHING I WANT TO HEAR

Tell me you had a rock collection
and hunted crayfish in streams.
Tell me you skipped stones. You
shot air rifles at squirrels and
picked your nose. Say you told
ghost stories and believed them.
You fought. You fell in love with girls
who didn't love you back. Say you lost
the house keys and broke in
through the back window or that
you broke in through the back window
anyway. Say you swam naked across
the lake. Say you never lit a match
on the first try. Say you burned
insects to watch their funeral pyres.
You were cruel or you were curious.
You weren't sure which you were more of.
Say you pretended to play guitar
until you could. You loved your dog.
You discovered the satisfaction
of rare meat. You lowered the hoop
on your basketball court. You drank
milk past its expiration date. Say
you invented new ways to defeat yourself.

## IV. THE FESTIVAL OF NEAR DEATH EXPERIENCES

put on your best shoes. there's blood
in the streets tonight, and some of it

is yours. pour the liquor. a toast
for the nights we almost brought back with us.

for every time we were not
the beneficiary of someone else's prayer.

it's never too late to learn:
where there's a needle, there must be

a cure nearby. see, you can't cheat death
but you can certainly make him work harder.

you can bring your own coffin to the party.
dress up nice, do your makeup

for the mortician, but don't imagine
your poker face is good enough.

death doesn't play. won't cloak
and dagger in the back of the sanctuary .

he's always been exactly what he is.
at the party since the DJ set up

catch death shimmying across the dancefloor
in a white fur coat. i saw him once

at the first break, lighting a cigarette
for my father. wink. what a smooth motherfucker.

eventually we're all going home with someone.
you can't cheat that. i'm going to go out dancing.

## V. DEBUNKING THE GOLDFISH

The common goldfish has a memory span of approximately three seconds.

The common goldfish   has a memory     span of   approximate
Did I say that already?

Sorry.
My whole life has been like walking into a room and forgetting why I'm there.
Wait
who are you?

Who are you?

There was this one time when
Nope.

There's never any time. I can't remember ever making any mistakes
so I have no anxieties about repeating them.

There's nobody with a pen and ledger looking over my shoulder
no chip on my shoulder. I don't have shoulders.

I don't have any obligations to history.

Folks talk about the past like it's
something they need to repair or escape from
and I don't really know what they mean. I can't even imagine...

Have you ever seen a memory?
What do they look like? Do they have rows of teeth?
Do they have little lanterns bobbing in the dark water?

I can't imagine anything larger than my own bowl,
so it's strange. The past is the only animal that will get bigger

if you spend too much time thinking about it.

I'll only get bigger if you put me in a bigger bowl. I make everyone happy
because I don't have any expectations to live up to.

Although, if I don't grow large enough my neighbors will
literally eat me. Isn't that gross?

Not like hermit crabs. Hermit crabs keep shedding their shells
and then they have to look back and see all the different places they've lived.

What's that called? Nostalgia? Regret? No. I don't speak it.

Goldfish don't have regrets which is why
you never see us swimming around with emotional baggage or regular baggage.

Wait! I think I saw a memory once! It looked just like me
and I could see it on the other side of the glass staring at me.
I didn't like it, so I turned around and then it disappeared.
It was that easy! Who knew? That past just goes away if you can't see it!

Do you think you can avoid things if you can't see them?

Do you think history is more like a boat you climb into or the wave that capsizes it?

Have you ever dropped a pebble into a fishbowl?
Some things just ripple
                    and ripple
                              and ripple.

I wonder if each ripple knows that it belongs to the one before it.
Maybe that's how it works. Maybe I belong to older, wiser moments.
Moments buried deep in me like fin rot.
Moments grown so big they no longer fit inside the bowl.

Maybe history is here with us all the time
even if we can't see it What?

What were we talking about?

## VI. ECHOCARDIOGRAPHY

Breathe in and hold, she says, the wand pressed up
against my ribs. Sometimes the air obstructs
the sound; sometimes a knife hides in the blood,
a blade slipped through the slits between the bones.
The monitor can show it all: the arc
and cavern of my chest, a beating heart
illuminated by the ultrasound.
The body is so shallow and so deep.
I watch my pulse and wonder at how much
we love the things we can't control. The fear
is that I'm either much too sick or else
not sick enough for them to know until
it kills me. Pointing at the screen, I ask,
Is that all normal? Please don't talk, she says.

## VII. MOON

as silent and holy as an empty church.
a polished row of pews. you, moon
in the sky, how do you do it?
your one-handed gravity
holding still the earth. astral magic trick,
you newly christened old god.
every family's forgotten dance is a scar
on your surface. memory like a bear trap.
worldfodder magnet. wise old sledgehammer
once smashed through our orbit longways.
we were just a pie cooling on the galactic
windowsill. now we say Light &
mean your face, stretched our whole lives
and once reached your shadow. pockmarked
queen of all ships. all flags. can't sing
a note of worship if it doesn't include
a word of pain. the night sky's
opening bell and serene last call,
nursing your craters like old wounds
nursing your craters like children.
your face held high and regal
through eons of the same steady bruise
and somehow you arrive to us with a bouquet
of escape of routes. i have so much
to learn from you, and not just about physics.
how long did it take you to learn
such luminescent confidence? your brilliant
backlit halo, the way you just float and move
everything, shine your own ligaments to dust.
when people say they love each other
to the You and back, is it about distance
or about damage? about some man's
lonely footprint? and what do we know
about damage next to you, anyway?

all our blood clots thick with time
but you have no winds to whisper
your name. sometimes the healing
does not rush through you. prehistoric ocean
or otherwise. there are no channels
you didn't cut yourself. no way to say Over
in the dead space. no one there to hear it
but a silent star.
                    and a billion other stars.

# VIII. LORAZEPAM

*AFTER SAM SAX*

When I was born
my mother said
my name, and that
is how I know
myself best.
The doctors only
give me names for
all the parts of me
that fail, and that
is how I know
I was not born
of pain. Was not
steeped in this
before all else.
I think sometimes
this is how it must feel
to be a bird
dropped from a wire.
To be a bird falling
and knowing all
the while this is not
what the body is for.
No coincidence, then
that insomnia mimics
prayer. The repetition.
The obsession
with voice regardless
of its efficacy.
*I'm going to get better*
God willing with both
hands and a blood pact.
With this remedy for
ringing church bells, this
small and brooding knot

slipped on the tongue.
And yes I fear
the name. I fear
the rings of benzene.
But more, I fear
what it means: that I
can't wait to swallow
my anxiety till it dissolves.

## IX.

I actually did it.
I actually called you a starfish
and not in a nice way (whatever that is).
I guess that makes me a crustacean,
an animal whose body is a cave
and its darkness all at once. An animal
more difficult to kill than is worth the time.
I've never been knocked around by love, only held
very tightly. I have a list of metaphors for the heart
and none of them are any good.

If you and I were still speaking these days
you'd laugh at this story. You'd ask me
which sea creature is most deserving of love.
And if not love, then what is worth changing
the body's circuitry. Lord, I never gave a fuck
about the phases of the moon until I met you,
and of all the currents pulling on the heart
I had to fall into this one.

Truthfully, I always thought my lineage
was that of submission. My father
came to this town on the heels of a woman
and you want me to move to Cleveland?
Cleveland? Even you know to pick up a lobster
from behind its claws. Maybe when I said
I was a crustacean, what I meant was
that I never learned how to surrender my body.

Call me any animal that thrives in saltwater.
If it's true that love comes from the heart
then we're all doomed anyway. After all,
the woman my father followed here is not
his wife. Is not my mother. We're all born

scuttling for the nearest pool of saline. Surrender
is the grandest thing the body does.
One day I hope to be dangerous
and pried open all at once.

## X. WHAT THE HEART IS

There's a tremor in my father's voice
when he speaks about the heart. He thinks it
is a shipwreck and the search for survivors
is a lost cause. Call out for the bodies.

When he speaks about the heart, I think of
a collection of stories, of who passed on
this lost cause and called it a body.
This is about his father, a man and

the collection of stories he passed on.
It's a pattern. It's a matter of genetics.
This is about my father, a man
I've spent a lot of time examining. Disaster

is a pattern. It's a matter of genetics
and history. I've been a fool for the heart.
I've spent a lot of time examining disaster,
how it struck my family like an instrument

of history. I've been a fool, for the heart
doesn't belong to any single one of us.
It struck my family like an instrument
and never left our bodies. The blood we share

doesn't belong to any single one of us.
It's extravenous, outside of the vein, though
it's never left my body, the blood we share
and the love I carry with it. Love, too

is extravenous, outside of the vein, and
in truth, my heart has always been
the love I carry with it. Our love, too,
at the same time. I wonder if

in truth, my heart has always been
a shipwreck and the search for survivors
at the same time. A wonder.
The tremor in my father's voice.

## XI. ELECTROPHYSIOLOGY

The good news is, your heart will always start
itself again after it stops, he says.
It's meant to be a comfort, just as much
as when you learn the circumstances of
your death down to the day. I wonder if
it's true only the good die young. If that's
the case, then all the old people I know
are assholes. Time is all it's ever been
about: The year I had to jerry-rig
my heart in place. Those fifteen seconds that
I spent beneath the surface. Ageing is
the same as dying gracefully, and I'm
already beautiful and doomed and full
of whatever it is that kills me.

## XII. IT'S THE SUMMER WE ARE SO SMALL

*CONTAINS LANGUAGE BORROWED FROM TONI MORRISON'S NOVEL* SONG OF SOLOMON

It's the summer we are so small

and your bonsai tree is ripped
out of the ground by some animal
probably. I want to make a joke
about selling the fetal tissue for research
but you're crying over this dead shrub
and other sadnesses, I assume
like how we care for things which are small
and dear to us and in return
they become uprooted.

What scares me about love is that
there's nowhere safe to put it.
I could build a vault of you
and never leave again. It would remain
there, protected, the way a mother's love
is concentrated in a single place.
How exhausting, you'd say to that.
What a terrible investment.

So how would you do it? Would you
grow and cultivate small life
that would not hurt you if it died?
Put all your eggs in different baskets
and don't count them before they hatch?
It's not the kind of question
that needs answering, though I have tried
to beg the words from the mouths of women.

You ever thought about how
a small wooden post is roped

around a sapling to keep it growing straight?
That's the kind of love I want
to provide for those who follow me.
Maybe it's an issue of grammar
and scale. Love isn't a seed we give each other
to bury in the dirt. Love is something
we're inside of together. Love is the dirt.
Watch. A small green stalk noses
into the light.

## XIII. FROM MY FATHER / FROM MY FUTURE SON

*AFTER OCEAN VUONG*

You've spent the whole year looking
at my life through a keyhole.

Telling my story, which you think belongs to you
just because you dipped yourself in a river
and came out breathing.

In this version, my voice is nothing
but an amateur death ripple.
Light refracting through dark water.

How careless
that you never considered it before.

Think of everything of mine you have
that has not tried to kill you.

Maybe that is what it means to be family.

To find yourself drowning
in my body.

That walking contradiction.
That one shared thing which separates.

Even your heart fails
in this story. It rips itself up in the telling.

Blind to the generosity of an open wound,
this selfish claim to blood.

When it does escape the vein
take the opportunity to consider yourself

part of something larger.

After all, the heart is just a series of passages.
If it plays a hand in love
it's only in the way people move through it
and back out again.

In the best-case scenario,
we damage our children in spectacular fashion.

In the worst, they leave this world
before we truly know them.

But this is not a séance. There is no ghost here.
No haunting.

Our parents do not ask us to carry them
but we carry them
anyway.

And if I belong to this story at all
it's only as the moral.

To convince you that history is circular
but not a circle.

To tell you how the heart pumps blood
to everyone
it's ever touched.

## XIV.

After the hospital
everything tastes a little like copper. I bite
my own tongue to know the metal,
a polluted creek running down my throat.
Listen: When I say my heart is broken
I don't mean there's a girl. I mean
I went down to the river. I did not
swim. I did not take off my shirt.
My chest is a faulty switchboard
and I can still feel wires for weeks
after the hospital. Listen: the heart
in this poem is not a metaphor. I tied
a penny to a length of fishing line
and swallowed it. The tiny god inside me
leaps as fish do when they're too close
to air. Have you ever been held
hostage by your own pulse?
Nothing shines as brightly
as a coin freshly minted
by someone about to kill you.
But listen: This poem is not about love
or if it is, it is only in the way
that every poem is about love.
It's about living with fear but living.
It's about the process through which
tributaries become oceans.
It's about going down to the river
and seeing a child and his father reeling
in their fishing line. A boy kicking straight
across the swimming hole. A girl
who is not at the water but floats
at the edges of each sentence
and I can feel her there. Just
there.

# XV. EXTRAVENOUS

My mother reminds me I'm a musician
as though that makes it truth
bright as a song or a story
what you want for your children
pulls in two different directions
Blood has some magic
that little sliver of red
connecting two halves in the body
My mother, the singer, says that
we're very much alike
we can both keep a tune
hum along to the past
maybe I do know a song or two
a sad, shared verse, but not
completely. A musician?
it's the truth, if only because
my parents have said it for years.
it feels realer than fact or
the music itself
. Now I'm starting to believe it
my throat, the bell of a trumpet
there's a single word for this
but it's read in two different ways:
Artery or vessel
two things at once
can make me stronger
a song and a son—

whenever I cut my hands
I picture my father offering me a cigarette
your children won't always want
their inheritance, a wound that
opens with the simplest blade.
beyond the obvious necromancy,
blood is a vein, but also a seam
a thin ribbon of light
my father and I
we battled fraternal sicknesses
and crack jokes about death
or the fluorescent hospital lights
my family, we know
how to finish each other's stories
it would be pure alchemy to say
I've never heard the ending.
I've been told it for so long that
at some point I just became
another tongue for the lie
all of us gathered into
a syringe or a riverbed
It's difficult for me to say
tempo or trauma.
Then again, maybe one thing can be
what kills me
and my father, both
wouldn't that be an ending?

# CLASSROOM GUIDE

Below are a few questions and considerations to discuss with students when teaching *XV* in your classroom:

What does the title *XV* mean to you? How do you pronounce it? How do you think it relates to the format and content of the collection?

The poems "Phlebotomy," "Echocardiography," and "Electrophysiology" are all loose sonnets that describe distinct medical procedures. What other instances of medical terminology can you find throughout the collection? Why do you think this concrete imagery is presented in juxtaposition to more figurative language?

The poem "Debunking the Goldfish" is a *persona poem*, a poetic form in which the author takes on the persona of a new character. Why do you think an author would choose to use a persona? If you wrote a persona poem, what character do you think you would use? It could be another person, an animal, or even an inanimate object.

The poem "What the Heart Is" is written as a *pantoum*, a poetic form in which certain lines repeat throughout the piece. In this example, the first line eventually ends up as the final line in the poem. Why do you think this poem in particular uses this form? How does the repetition of lines reinforce the theme of the piece or the collection at large?

Throughout the collection, there are several instances of language and metaphors that relate to water, rivers, or oceans. How does the image of moving water relate to the collection's themes of history and inheritance? Can you think of other imagery or metaphors that might be used to similar effect?

The final poem in the collection, "Extravenous," is a *contrapuntal*, a poetic form in which two columns can be read vertically as separate pieces or horizontally as a single poem. Why do you think this poem is written as a contrapuntal, and what does this decision say about the collection as a whole?

# ACKNOWLEDGEMENTS

So very grateful to J. K. Fowler and the staff of Nomadic Press for giving this collection a home. Thanks to *Bird's Thumb*, *Oatmeal Magazine*, *sPARKLE & bLINK*, and *voicemail poems* for previously publishing some of these pieces in their earlier iterations.

This collection would not have been possible without the support and encouragement of so many wonderful communities: West Club, DYWC, C4, the Dopenhagen, 142 Cross, WeSLAM, Mango House, the Noodles/Spatzle, Oxbow, the Bay Area poets, the Muse, the Berkeley Slam teams and organizers. You have raised and continue to raise me.

Love and gratitude for my friends who have given their time to some of these pieces: Grace Aheron, Kaylen Baker, Abe Becker, Tatyana Brown, Collin Edmonds, Reggie Edmonds, Scott Farmer, Em Kianka, Nate Mondschein, Victoria Morgan, Peter Myers, Kay Nilsson, Joey Page, Sean Porter, Mike Rosen, sam sax, Maya Sisneros, Javi Somejo, Jaz Sufi, and Emily Weitzman. I am so lucky to know you.

To my partner, Mel: Joyous gardner. Forever reader. Best friend. What else can we grow together?

To my family, Peter, Susan, Ross, Jess, and Evan: you are the tributaries that run into all my work. I cannot thank you enough. Dad: you gave me the music. This is for you.

**ZACH GOLDBERG** is a North Carolina-born writer, educator, and arts organizer. He attended Wesleyan University, where he co-facilitated and competed with WeSLAM, Wesleyan's nationally-ranked poetry slam team in 2012 and 2013. He lived in the Bay Area for six years and was a member of the 2018 and 2019 Berkeley Slam Teams. Zach's work has appeared in *voicemail poems*, *Bird's Thumb*, *Oatmeal Magazine,* and elsewhere. Professionally, Zach has worked as an ice cream maker, a stage manager, and an arts administrator, and he currently lives in Minneapolis with his partner and their growing collection of board games. IG: @gach_zoldberg